Written by Marie Farré
Illustrated by Dominique Thibault

Specialist Adviser:
Brigitte Ganiol-Coppin
Historian

ISBN 0-944589-06-5
First U.S. Publication 1988 by
Young Discovery Library
217 Main St. · Ossining, NY 10562

©*1985 by Editions Gallimard*
Translated by Sarah Matthews
English text © 1986 by Moonlight Publishing Ltd.
Special thanks to Aileen Buhl

YOUNG DISCOVERY LIBRARY

Long Ago
in a Castle

What was it like living
safe behind castle walls?

YOUNG DISCOVERY LIBRARY

Hastings Castle in England

Have you ever seen a castle?
Most castles nowadays are more or less in ruins.
When they were first built they were strong and powerful, gazing down from their hilltops onto the countryside around.

The lord lived in a castle, and the people from the villages nearby would shelter there in times of danger.
Life was much more dangerous then, with bands of thieves and outlaws, wild animals and, all too often, war, when the lords of the castles fought each other.

Gutenfels Castle
in Germany

How long have people been building castles?

Castles were first built over a thousand years ago. They began by being simple wooden towers with a ditch around them.

Wooden castle

12th century stone castle

By the end of the 11th century, some castles were built of stone. At times the walls were 25 feet thick.

Building a castle could take 40 years! A village for the workmen would grow up around it.

Some 15th century castles were built like palaces.

Avila, a fortified town in Spain

Loches
Castle
in France

Some of the lords were very powerful. They were complete masters over whole regions. Often they owned several castles. Sometimes their castles were bigger than the king's!

You can still find remains of these castles in Britain, France, Germany Spain, Italy, Switzerland... None of them are entirely alike, but

Peñafiel Castle, in Spain

they all have ramparts, a drawbridge and a strong tower called a keep.

Castel del Monte, in Italy

1. Ditch or moat
2. Rampart
3. Battlements
4. Crenellations
5. Wall walk
6. Arrow slit
7. Portcullis
8. Drawbridge
9. Curtain wall protecting the keep
10. Openings through which stones and
    boiling oil could be dropped on the enemy.
11. Keep

12

Shall we take a look inside?

The first problem would be to get in. You would wait for the drawbridge (1) to be lowered, before crossing the moat, which might be very deep. Watch out for the sharp points on the portcullis (2)!

There are soldiers on guard on the ramparts, protected by the crenellations. They can peep around to watch the enemy. There aren't any windows in the walls, are there? Only narrow slits. Archers firing arrows out of them were protected, while the enemy couldn't see them.

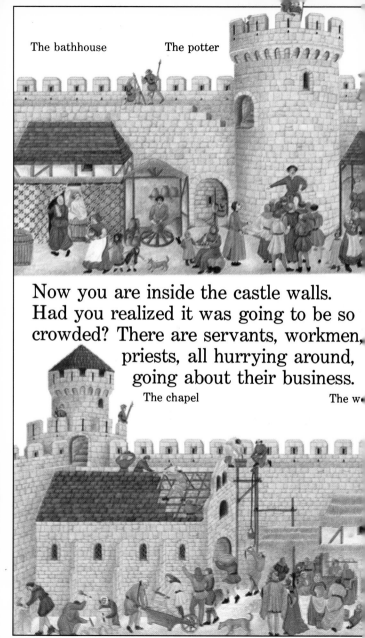

The bathhouse   The potter

Now you are inside the castle walls.
Had you realized it was going to be so
crowded? There are servants, workmen,
priests, all hurrying around,
going about their business.

The chapel   The w

The forge

here are pigs, dogs and hens scratching
d wandering about. It's as busy as a
all town on market day, isn't it?

nife grinder   A traveling peddler

Where does the lord live?

The lord and his family live in the keep, the strongest part of the castle. The door is on the first floor, with a ladder leading to it which can be drawn up when there's an attack. It is very dark inside. In the evening, blazing torches light the rooms and the great hall, while a huge fire keeps everyone warm.

These are the crests of some of the noble families. The lion represents strength; the cross stands for Christianity.

There is very little furniture. In the bedroom a chest where clothes are folded away is used as a seat as well. The storeroom is on the ground floor, as well as a tunnel to escape by should

the need arise...On the top floor there is a guardroom for the soldiers.

Passing the evening playing chess.

What does the lady of the castle do?

Only some windows had glass, it was so expensive.

She looks after the household, and is in charge of affairs if the lord is not there. She is responsible for provisions and for organizing meals. She knows about herbs, and how to use them in nursing the sick. Sometimes she'll go hunting with her falcon, or watch a tournament. It was rare for people in the Middle Ages to be able to read, as the lady in the picture is doing.

The lady teaches her daughters to weave. Little girls are engaged to be married very young. They become wives at fifteen.

A boy leaves his mother when he's eight years old. He may be a page in a neighboring castle or he may go to school in a monastery. Being a page meant learning to be obedient and helpful. Boys have names like Henry, William, John... Girls are called Anne, Blanche, Eleanor...

Travelers are welcome at the castle, particularly if they can tell of interesting adventures to pass the long evenings.

The lord and his people

The peasants work on the lord's land. In return each family receives a house and some land on which they can grow their own crops. The peasants' life is centered on the castle: the lord's soldiers protect them from raiders, they grind their wheat in the lord's mill, and bake their bread in the lord's oven. In time of war they can take shelter in the castle.

All this costs money: the lord collects taxes from the peasants so that he can pay his soldiers and feed his servants.

The lord's seal
with his coat
of arms

Travelers using the roads an
bridges on the lord's lan
had to pay a to

Stocks

As well as protecting the peasants, the lord kept an eye on less powerful lords, who followed him in war. They were called his vassals.

The lord's word was law. If you did not obey him, you could end up in the dungeons. Sometimes people were put in the stocks: fastened by their hands or feet they couldn't duck the rotten vegetables or stones that people threw at them.

A village nestling under the castle walls.

A flail for beating the grain, and a basket for sieving it.

In the village

People and animals all lived together in the cottages. Sometimes the animals had a room downstairs, while the people slept above them, kept warm by the animals' bodies. As soon as winter was over, the peasants were out working in the fields. They sowed the grain, sheared the sheep, and harvested the crops.

When the harvest was over there was a big festival — the castle had enough food to last through next winter! But the peasants did not always have enough left after paying the lord all they owed him. They would search for nuts and wild berries to have something extra to eat.

The castle is busy getting ready for the feast. A whole pig is roasting on a spit over the fire in the smoky kitchen. In the Hall servants scurry about putting up trestle tables to seat all the guests.

What will there be to eat?

Roast pig, eel pie, venison, chunks of bread, spicy sauces. And perhaps, as it's a special occasion, a roast peacock.

Knife, forks, a hunk of bread for a plate.

or dessert there
will be fruit pies,
tarts, and puddings
made with cream and
honey. There will be
ale, cider and spiced
wine to drink.

Cups and plates are made of wood, or
pewter, and sometimes of silver, or gold.

The feast will last for hours.

Jugglers, acrobats, dancing bears and
monkeys amuse the guests. There are
traveling musicians, called minstrels,
playing tunes for people to dance to,
and troubadours to sing songs of love
and bravery.

27

How does the lord go hunting?

He enjoys hunting with a falcon. The bird flies up, spots a rabbit, dives down onto it, and then flies back to the lord's gloved hand.

He may also shoot hares and pheasants with a bow and arrow.

Boar hunting with spears

picnic during
hunt. Hot food
provided from
traveling
kitchen.

When the lord goes hunting with his hounds, he rides on horseback. The dogs run ahead and track down a deer or a boar. They chase it for mile after mile until the hunted animal is worn out, then the lord finishes it off with a spear. The lord hunts for fun, but also to provide food for the table, and to kill animals, like wolves and wild boar, which might hurt his sheep and his crops. The peasants are only allowed to hunt small animals such as rabbits, which they catch in traps. These little animals give them fresh meat to eat and fur to wear.

A knight's most precious possessions were his sword and his war-horse.

After being a page, the young boy becomes a squire, a servant to a knight, and then at 18 he is made a knight himself. Kneeling in church, he makes the knight's promise: to keep his word, defend the weak, and be a good Christian. Then he buckles on his sword and mounts his war-horse, ready to go to battle for his lord.

Shield

Lance

Knights wore armor, made of metal rings closely linked together. It was very strong, and very, very heavy, weighing over 22 pounds.

Some knights wore steel armor
which was so heavy they had to be
lifted onto their horses. Even the
horses wore armor!

Everyone has gathered to watch the tournament.

Knights have come from far and near to fight each other. Some champions travel from castle to castle, challenging other knights.

Each knight wears his own special coat of arms so that people can recognize him. The winner of the tournament receives a prize from the noblest of the ladies. In the evening they all feast in the castle together.

Crossbow

The castle is under siege.

Surrounded by enemies, the people in the castle can't escape. They have a lot of food stored. Perhaps they can wait it out. But the leader of the enemy army decides to attack. He orders logs to be thrown into the moat to fill it so that great towers on wheels can be pushed against the walls. Soldiers run up with ladders. Others swing a huge pole, called a battering ram, to try and make a hole to charge through. From the top of the walls, the defending soldiers rain down arrows on the attackers, and shower them with stones and boiling oil. Who do you think will win?

The attackers dig tunnels under the walls to get into the castle.

O, young Lochinvar is come out of the west,
Through all the wide border his steed was the best;
And save his good broadsword, he weapons had nor
He rode all unarmed, and he rode all alone.
So faithful in love, and so dauntless in war,
There never was knight like the young Lochinvar.

from Lochinvar
by Sir Walter Scott